Original title:
Roots in Tiny Pots

Copyright © 2025 Creative Arts Management OÜ
All rights reserved.

Author: Elliot Harrison
ISBN HARDBACK: 978-1-80581-710-9
ISBN PAPERBACK: 978-1-80581-237-1
ISBN EBOOK: 978-1-80581-710-9

Tethered to Tomorrow

In a pot that's far too small,
A sprout dreams of the great big hall.
With hopes to touch the sky so high,
But first, it must learn how to try.

A twig bends under life's big scheme,
Yet it plots and schemes, chasing a dream.
With water and sun, it grows with glee,
But oh, what a sight—a dancing pea!

The snails all take their slow parade,
While our little sprout, in green, is made.
It wiggles and jiggles, not feeling shy,
As it greets the breeze with a tiny sigh.

In this pot of dreams and mud galore,
It hopes for more than just the floor.
With laughter it whispers, "Watch me bloom!"
Just a tiny plant, but full of zoom!

Embracing the Compact

In a pot so snug, my dreams are small,
I wonder how I'll fit them all.
With leaves that giggle and stems that sway,
I dance with joy in this humble bay.

My neighbors, the herbs, are quite the crew,
They joke about growth when there's hardly room.
Yet here we thrive, with quirky flair,
In this tiny home, we breathe the air.

Essence of Expansion

My cactus pricks a sense of cheer,
It's got the spirit of a pioneer.
A flower blooms, all bright and bold,
In a spot where the sun isn't cold.

While others spread wide and far with pride,
We giggle and wiggle, we won't hide.
In our snug plot, we'll plot and scheme,
Tiny but mighty, it's our dream team!

Breaking Ground in Limited Land

In this pot of dreams, I stretch my legs,
I wiggle my ferns, and sometimes beg.
The soil's too tight, but that won't stop,
I'll wear my best bloom, I'll never flop!

A tiny tomato waves hello,
"Join the fun, put on a show!"
We're like a circus all crammed in,
With laughter and joy, the real win.

The Promise Inside

In a ceramic shell, we find our way,
Giggling buds at the end of the day.
While the world may say we're stuck in a jam,
We whisper secrets like a silly exam.

With dreams of gardens we'll never see,
Yet full of laughter, wild and free.
The promise inside, not bound by size,
In tiny pots, we reach for the skies.

Sheltered Yet Thriving

In a pot so small, yet dreams can bloom,
A cactus in a corner, claiming all the room.
With its prickly charm and size so neat,
It giggles at the daisy, who's feeling beat.

A sunflower standing tall, but barely a height,
Telling jokes to the lily, who giggles in delight.
"Why so small?" wonders the proud old tree,
"Because I got the sunshine, just you wait and see!"

The Elegance of Containment

Elegance in a cup, oh what a sight,
A plant in a teacup, feeling just right.
"I'm a fine dining experience," it says with a grin,
"Watch out, world! This is where fun begins!"

A tiny fern, slyly peeking from its case,
Declares, "I'm a trendsetter in this small space!"
Who needs a garden, when style's in the pot?
Get your own little nook, like it or not!

Beneath the Surface

Beneath the soil, a party's in play,
Where critters and worms dance the day away.
"Watch our tiny Earth, it's a saucy affair!"
Said the roots to each other, with a wink and a glare.

They whisper sweet secrets, while seeking the light,
And giggle at plants, reaching with all their might.
"Why grow so big? It's the fun that we seek!"
They jive in their spots, playing hide and seek!

The Microcosm of Growth

In a world so small, things grow with grace,
A radish in a vessel, claiming its space.
"Look at me, I'm spicy!" it cheekily roars,
While carrots chuckle, discussing their chores.

A tiny tomato boasts, "I'm small but I'm sweet!"
While peas in their pods all have fun in their seat.
In miniature realms, all flavors are grand,
Growing, thriving, together they stand!

Budding Beneath the Surface

In tiny homes, they dance and sway,
Dreaming of fields where they could play.
Chasing sunshine with all their might,
Yet here they are, a comical sight.

They poke their heads and stretch their leaves,
Through little cracks, like mischievous thieves.
With every inch, they push and shove,
Yearning for skies they're dreaming of.

Nature's Little Guardians

In pots so small, they wear their capes,
With tiny fists and sprouting shapes.
Guardians of laughter, in green parade,
Saving the world from a boring shade.

They trade tall tales of mountains high,
While sipping dew from the morning sky.
A hero's tale in a tiny space,
Where each leaf wears a cheerful face.

Strength in Smallness

Who needs a forest when you've got flair?
These little champs are light as air.
Strutting their stuff in the sunlight glow,
Tiny but mighty, putting on a show!

They laugh at storms with a cheeky grin,
"Try your best, you'll never win!"
With roots so clever, they hold on tight,
Creating joy in their pocket-sized fight.

The Quiet Bloom

In hushed corners, a giggle erupts,
As petals unfold and bravely disrupts.
Quietly blooming in their small domain,
Making the mundane feel less of a pain.

They whisper secrets to passing ants,
While dreaming of brighter flowered plants.
Beneath the surface, they chuckle and cheer,
Turning the commonplace into delight here!

Petal by Petal

Small blooms dance with glee,
A little pot they see.
They laugh and twist with mirth,
In this tiny patch of earth.

Whispers float on sunny beams,
Living out their silly dreams.
Each petal wears a silly hat,
Chatting with a nearby cat.

A ladybug joins the fun,
Underneath the warming sun.
They leap from leaf to leaf, oh wow,
Who knew plants could party now?

In their mini, green domain,
They jest and joke, but none in vain.
With roots so cozy, snug, and tight,
They find the joy in every bite!

The Weight of a Feather

A feather falls, what a sight,
It lands on leaves, oh, what a plight!
The little pots begin to shake,
As if they're all awake from cake.

Giggles echo in the breeze,
As petals sway with such great ease.
"Is it my weight?" one leaf will cry,
While dandelions all float by.

The tiny pots begin to sway,
"Look at us, we won the day!"
While worms do somersaults below,
Cheering on the feathery show.

In laughter's grip, they sing aloud,
Together with their silly crowd.
Life's a party when you're this small,
Who knew a feather could cause a brawl?

Flora's Invitation

Dear buds in pots, come one, come all,
To Flora's bash, it'll be a ball!
With cookies made from soil and sun,
And lettuce wraps; oh, what a fun!

The daisies twirl in fancy dress,
While cacti practice their finesse.
"Who brings the punch?" asks goofy thyme,
"I forgot again, it's party time!"

With petals fluffed, they all arrive,
The tiniest crew, so full of jive.
Chanting songs of joy so sweet,
While dancing dandelions treat.

"Let's party hard, but not too long,
Or we might just forget our song!"
With laughter echoing in the air,
Flora's pot show is beyond compare!

Life's Quiet Conquests

In pots so small, they stake their claim,
With every sprout, it's quite the game.
They poke and prod their tiny space,
Making conquerors of gentle grace.

"Here's a weed!" a petal shouts,
"A worthy foe, let's see who sprouts!"
Of course, the dandelion's grin,
Makes winning feel like such a sin.

With worms as judges, keen and wise,
They rate the tallest in the skies.
Who knew such tiny could inspire,
A garden full of silly fire?

In quiet moments, laughter grows,
Through every twist, and turn, and pose.
Life's a jest among the best,
In little pots, they find their quest!

Tenders of the Soil

Digging with glee, they dance around,
Sprinkling their laughs into the ground.
Tiny hands pat the earth in a jig,
Who knew dirt had such a big gig?

Worms wiggled out, a sight to behold,
They giggle and shout, 'We're nugget of gold!'
Each little sprout is a friend not a foe,
Growing together, a pot full of show!

Life Cradled in Clay

A pot so small, but dreams are large,
Sprouts peek out, ready to charge.
Pushing their heads through the clay so thick,
They plot their escape, their masterful trick.

Sunshine beams down, making them grin,
'We're tiny and mighty, let the games begin!'
With raindrops to drink and dirt for a bed,
Who knew little buds had so much in their head?

Seeds of Resilience

Planted in pots, a motley crew,
With dirt-flecked hats and a bright green hue.
They chuckle at storms that come on the scene,
Shaking their leaves like a fun trampoline.

When snails come to visit, they throw up their hands,
'Oh please, Mr. Snail, don't ruin our plans!'
But the tiny seeds know, they're built like a tank,
Strong against chaos, full of green prank.

Heartbeats of the Undergrowth

In the heart of the pots, a fiesta thrives,
Underneath the soil, every critter jives.
With roots that tickle and sprigs that play,
A botanical party in their own little way.

They giggle and wiggle in their cozy nook,
Turning the dirt into a cook-book.
Each little sprout a dancer so bold,
Spinning tales of wonder, bright and gold.

Fragility and Fortitude

In a pot so small, it wobbles near,
A sprout peeks out, and we all cheer.
With sunshine dreams and dancing sun,
It struggles hard, but it's just begun.

A sneeze might send it back to sleep,
Yet here it stands, no time for sheep.
With little leaves like tiny hands,
It waves 'hello' as it understands.

In a world so big, it's a tiny champ,
And who needs space? Just plug the lamp.
With water drops and little hugs,
It grows up strong, dodging all the bugs.

Blossoms from a Pinch of Earth

A pinch of soil, a dash of luck,
In this little jar, it's out of pluck.
A bonsai dream in a coffee cup,
It pokes its head and says, "What's up?"

Dancing petals like confetti bursts,
In this tiny realm, the flower thirsts.
No need for gardens grand and wide,
Just humor found in this playful ride.

The bees look down, confused, bemused,
How can such joy come in a snooze?
Yet here we laugh, and watch it grow,
In a pot on the shelf, just putting on a show.

Tiny Tapestries of Growth

Tangled greens weave a carpet tight,
Stitching stories in the morning light.
In a little cup, a forest dreams,
With giggles shared and silly schemes.

Each leaf a tale, each bud a pun,
If only they could join in on the fun.
With every inch, they cheer, they leap,
Tiny tapestries, oh secrets they keep!

A matchbox garden with colors galore,
Who knew such joy could fit through the door?
A minuscule world, yet it's so profound,
In these small lives, hilarity's found.

Sheltered Growth

In a quirky pot, where laughter bakes,
Sits a little plant that shimmies and shakes.
With walls so thick but a heart so wide,
It tickles the sun and dances with pride.

Sheltered from storms, it pokes its nose,
What keeps it up? Well, nobody knows!
It snacks on sunshine, sips on the rain,
While practicing jokes about it's tiny gain.

With every slight breeze, it sways with glee,
Who needs the vast when you can be free?
In space so snug, it thrives with flair,
A tiny plant with the spirit to share.

Expansive Dreams

In a teacup realm, ambitions grow,
A dreamer's heart in a pot's soft glow.
It dreams of forests, rain, and more,
Yet here it is, just waiting for the floor.

With roots so bold but hardly seen,
It fakes a smile, like it's in a scene.
"Oh, to be a tree!" it loudly sighs,
As it rolls its leaves and blinks its eyes.

A clover heart's a world in disguise,
With all the pranks and little lies.
In half a cup, it thinks real big,
Nah, size doesn't matter, as it strikes a jig.

Seeds of Promise

Little seeds in their cozy beds,
Dreaming big with tiny heads.
They wiggle and squirm trying to grow,
In snug little spaces, putting on a show.

Each night they whisper, 'We can't be beat!'
While dodging the cat and avoiding her feet.
They daydream of daisies, and cornfields wide,
But for now, they're just happy inside.

Lush Life in Closed Corners

In the corner of the kitchen, a dance so sly,
Parsley jives with thyme, oh my!
Basil's got moves, it's a tight little groove,
In their little domain, they've got nothing to prove.

With every sprinkle of water, they cheer with glee,
'We're the lush life, can't you see?'
The sun peeks in, they do a quick spin,
In their tiny pot, they're the kings of the din.

Stunted Yet Striving

Some say they're stunted, but what do they know?
With determination, they put on a show.
A sprout with pizazz, a leaf full of sass,
In overgrown dreams, they still manage to pass.

Each centimeter fought with a personality bright,
Challenging gravity, oh what a sight!
They laugh at the weeds, belittling their plight,
In their small little world, they shine out of spite.

Potent Intent in Petty Planters

In pots that are petty, intent they hold,
A garden of humor, all of them bold.
With cheeky little grins, they sprout with delight,
Who says small can't mean a victory bright?

They trade jokes with the soil, a giggle or two,
'Can your roots do the tango?' a clever little cue.
In the dance of the sun, they sway and they cheer,
For every tiny planter, there's joy to endear.

Fragile Beginnings

In a pot too small for a sprout,
The plant sorta whispers, "What's this about?"
Wiggling and jiggling, it tries to break free,
But finds it's stuck like a bee in a tea.

With dreams of a garden, oh so grand,
It stretches for sunshine, but only gets sand.
A tiny leaf sighs, "I need my space,"
While neighborly weeds laugh, filling the place.

Small Containers

In a cup of old tea, a seed starts to bob,
It dreams of the world but only a blob.
Challenging limits in a tiny game,
It rolls with the punches, never feeling shame.

"I'm not just a seed! I'm a mighty tree!"
While peering at marigolds looking so free.
The next-door herbs giggle with glee,
As our little plant ponders, "What will I be?"

Grand Hopes

Tiny plans hatch like dreams at night,
In pots far too small, but oh, what a sight!
With high hopes and ambitions, they reach for the sky,
While teetering on edges, they wobble and fly.

"One day I'll grow tall, and you all will see!"
The little sprout shouts, "Just wait, trust me!"
But the pot snickers, "You're part of a team,"
As the others respond, "Hey, don't be so extreme!"

The Beauty Beneath the Surface

Under the soil, it's lively and bright,
Little critters dance deep into the night.
When digging for treasure, how odd it seems,
All the roots giggle, exchanging their dreams.

"I'm a garden warrior!" claims one with pride,
While others just chuckle, "Come on, don't hide!"
But the dirt holds them close, as they twist and they twine,
Creating a party, all secretly fine.

Growth in Limited Spaces

In a pot of old clay, a challenge remains,
Where sprouting ambitions dance through the pains.
Each leaf takes a bow, and the others just stare,
As they all wonder, "Do I really care?"

But lo and behold, with laughter and glee,
They stretch up and out, as sprightly as can be.
In a tiny estate, they open their hearts,
Making tiny pot dreams into giant works of art.

Transitions in Miniature

In a pot not quite so grand,
A cactus dreams of desert sand.
It stretches tall, though just a sprout,
Wishing for more room, no doubt!

A tiny fern in emerald hue,
Claims the whole kitchen as its view.
With leaves that wave like little flags,
It's ready to pop up and brag!

A sunflower whispers, "I'm a star!"
But friends, they say, "Just stay where you are!"
With petals bright, it makes do well,
In a pot that's only an inch from hell!

The herbs all plot their nightly spree,
Chasing dreams of spice and glee.
But every morn, it's clear to see,
They're stuck in soil, oh dearie me!

The Scale of Potential

In a cup, a radish sings,
"I'm more than just a thing with rings!"
"Give me ground, I'll rise and shine,
But here I dwell, just biding time!"

The carrot's grumble sounds like thunder,
In this cup, it's going under.
"I want to grow and stretch out wide,
Not be a snack on the side!"

A pea pod dreams of climbing high,
But in this pot, it's doomed to sigh.
"Let's make a plan for a wild escape,
From this confinement, that's no great shape!"

In every nook, they find delight,
Joking about their silly plight.
Nature laughs, watching them dance,
In small vessels, they take their chance!

Garden of the Underdog

In a dish, a dandelion stands brave,
Dreaming of fields, wild and wave.
"I'm the underdog, can't you see?
I've got the spirit of a mighty tree!"

A lonely thyme in a teacup waits,
Yearning for gardens and bigger plates.
It hums a tune, blending flavors right,
Hoping someday to join the bite!

A lazy basil gives a yawn,
"Oh, to be in the early dawn!"
While snuggled tight in its little space,
It dreams of salads, what a race!

These tiny plants, with hearts so bold,
Make magic in pots, stories told.
Laughter echoes in this plant brigade,
Every small leaf has a role played!

Nooks of Nature

In a nook, a pot does grin,
A squash says, "Let the fun begin!"
"I'm mean to be a dinner star,
But for now, I'm just bizarre!"

An acorn's plotting, "Just you wait!"
"I troll this pot, but I feel great!"
"I'll sprout a tree, in time you'll see,
Just need a little sympathy!"

A peppy pepper dreams in green,
"I'll spice things up, know what I mean?"
"Right now I'm tiny, but full of zest,
In this corner, I'll be the best!"

These nooks of nature, where joy is rife,
Show us all the fun in life.
Beneath the sun in cramped little plots,
They plot and laugh, those silly tots!

Castles in Containers

In a cup there's a fortress, quite small,
Knights made of peas, they stand tall.
A moat of tomato soup surrounds,
As they battle with forks for food crowns.

Little towers of carrots poke out,
While radish soldiers scream and shout.
The peas declare a royal feast,
In their kingdom, they are the least.

On mango slices, they have their fun,
Sending cucumber spies to run.
Each tiny castle holds a tale,
Of veggie warriors, who never fail.

At dusk they dance under the light,
With popcorn cannons serving delight.
A mini realm where giggles grow,
In containers where silliness flows.

Hidden Growth

Beneath a lid, they're plotting schemes,
Chives whisper secrets, selling dreams.
Tomatoes in shades of pink and red,
Vow to be more than just a salad's spread.

A carrot has visions, tall as the sky,
As cabbages giggle, oh my, oh my!
In their cozy pots, dreams take flight,
Growing big hopes in the dead of night.

The herbs play hide and seek with the sun,
In their green world, they spin and run.
A sprinkle of humor, a dash of cheer,
With every watering can, they persevere.

These tiny plots hold wonders untold,
Where laughter and greens go hand in fold.
So beware the pots, full of surprise,
They might just bloom into comical pies!

Fragility of Anchorage

A sprout is anchored in a pet dish,
Dreaming of oceans, like a fish.
Though small and dainty, it stands tall,
Rooted in laughter, ready for all.

A breeze might toss it, a giggle here,
A leaf does a shimmy, drawing near.
It sways and bends, oh what a twist,
In its tiny world, nothing's amiss.

Stability's tricky for those who grow,
In pots so small, their antics flow.
Yet here they thrive, with a smile and glee,
Holding court at their miniature jubilee.

Fragile yet fierce, they dance with grace,
In their little laps of space.
Each tender sprout seeks its stride,
Finding joy where silliness resides.

Miniature Gardens

In bowls of joy, they take their stand,
With thimble-trees and a dandelion band.
Pebbles for boulders, tiny stones,
Each plant a king, claiming its thrones.

A daisy looks at a dandelion proud,
While violets giggle, gathering a crowd.
They dance to the tunes of a tiny breeze,
In this plush paradise, they do as they please.

Gnomes made of clay keep watch by night,
Wishing for sunshine, oh what a sight!
While potted zucchinis play hide and seek,
With a wink and a nod, they never speak.

In pots full of laughter, dreams set sail,
As colorful petals tell a tale.
With each little sprout, joy takes its place,
In gardens so small, there's no need for space.

Mighty Spirits

Tiny beans dream of being big,
Waltzing around with a little jig.
Potted plants boast of their might,
In a world so small, it feels just right.

In each little plant, a spirit thrives,
With whispers of fun, their laughter derives.
A bachelor button thinks it's quite grand,
Claiming the pot like a rock star band.

Tiny pots hold a will so bold,
Where stories of triumph are ever told.
With playful whimsy, the seeds unite,
Creating a ruckus in sheer delight.

The mighty spirits laugh with glee,
In their mini kingdom, wild and free.
Join the dance, where humor's a must,
For the smallest of gardens, bring joyous thrust!

Breaching Boundaries

In a tiny pot, he thinks he's grand,
With dreams of jungles, oh so unplanned.
His little leaves wave, bold as a flag,
Yet the neighbor's cat sneezes, oh what a drag!

He stretches and twists, in vivid display,
Challenging fences, making them sway.
The sun casts laughter on his green parade,
But here comes the dog—oh, what a charade!

The winds giggle softly, tickling his base,
As he spies the world, oh what a race!

The Clutch of Nature

A bud in a cup, filled with pure glee,
He whispers to droplets, let's dance, just us three!
With a wink and a wiggle, he starts to create,
A circus of colors, it's never too late.

The sunlight peeks in, as if to partake,
While ants are his audience, for laughter's sake.
He juggles his leaves, he's ready to roll,
But oops—a little worm just stole the whole show!

A puddle of water splashes forth giddy,
Leaving him soaked—but boy, isn't he witty!

Whispering Green in Concrete

A sprout in a crack, what a sight to behold,
With dreams of adventure, both daring and bold.
Kicking up dust with a cheeky little grin,
He shouts to the pigeons, "Let the fun begin!"

The sidewalks do giggle, while rain starts to play,
As he wiggles and jiggles in his leafy ballet.
A spritz from a puddle, he gives a quick sigh,
'Just my luck,' he moans—'I'm the little guy.'

But laughter erupts from the clouds up above,
As sunbeams cascade, showering him with love.

Hopeful Sprigs Amongst Stone

In a kingdom of pavement, a hero stands small,
With dreams of becoming the tallest of all.
He stretches his limbs, a frisky young sprite,
Challenging boulders, oh, what a sight!

The gravel around him snickers and chirps,
As he spins and hops like a dancer who jerks.
Curious spiders pay him a visit,
Giggles and wiggles, oh isn't it exquisite?

As raindrops descend, he's ready to play,
With puddles for pools, he'll splash just all day!

The Elysium of the Small

In a pot so small, a sprout peeks out,
Waving hello without a doubt.
Sipping light like a cocktail treat,
Tiny dancer on its tiny feet.

Each morning sun, a disco ball,
Jumps and jumps till it might fall.
Chasing shadows in a single breeze,
A tiny sage, at ease with ease.

The neighbors laugh, they can't believe,
A little plant with dreams to weave.
In this cramped space, it finds its way,
Making mischief every day.

Its leaves pretend to be a fan,
As it winks like a tiny man.
Who knew that joy could be so small?
Dancing here, we're having a ball!

Blossoming Through the Barricade

Two stones chat, they say, 'What's this?
A flower sprouting, something we miss?'
With a grin, it stretches wide,
Defiant little thing, with pride!

'Excuse me, rocks, I need some sun,
Can't stop me now, I'm just having fun!'
Through the cracks, it finds its way,
Showing the world it's here to stay.

Bouncing leaves on a breeze so free,
Color popping with glee, oh me!
Scolding stones, saying 'Move aside,
I'm the star of this joyride!'

So they chuckle and decide to cheer,
For the pot of soil, the best frontier.
In this world with rocks and mud,
A little bloom, like a wild flood!

Growth Against the Odds

In a jar of jam, what's that I see?
A sprout grins back and looks at me.
'You never thought I'd throw this party,
Yet here I am, oh so hearty!'

The lid's a roof, but who needs air?
This plant is cozy without a care.
A tiny King upon its throne,
All alone, yet never alone.

Jamming out like it's the best hit,
Wiggling, giggling, not one bit quit.
With sugar dreams and fruit-filled nights,
It spreads its leaves, oh what delights!

Next to the window, it catches light,
Look at it now, what a funny sight!
Against all odds, it finds a laugh,
A tiny sprout on a royal path!

Hope Held Tightly

In a mug with stripes, what a twist!
A stubborn green, it can't resist.
'Though it's cramped, I'm feeling grand,
This coffee cup is my dreamland!'

Friends nearby, they frown and stare,
'What's that? A plant? Isn't it rare?'
But no! With soil, and heart, it beams,
A little hero, living dreams!

Cheerful chatter, it sips the dew,
Saying 'Life's short, so here's what's true:
I'll grow and sway with all my might,
In this tiny space, I'll shine so bright!'

So cheers to hope, both near and far,
In a little place, we can be a star.
With a smile and a wink, it stays alive,
In this funny mess, we all will thrive!

The Spirit of the Small

In a pot so small, with dreams so bright,
Little plants dance, in morning light.
They wiggle and giggle, quite a show,
Tiny leaves wave, 'Look at us grow!'

A tomato's a joke, but oh so sweet,
Living on laughter and scraps of beet.
With roots that are cozy, no need for space,
In their little world, they've found their place.

Echoes of Green

In miniature homes, the whispers flow,
Tiny greens boast, 'Come, watch us glow!'
Each leaf has a tale, a giggle to lend,
Sassy little sprouts, on them we depend.

With a sprinkle of joy and a pinch of fun,
They tease the sun, saying, 'Let's run!'
A sprout's witty jibe, a laugh shared wide,
In pots snug and cozy, where they take pride.

In the Shade of a Lid

Beneath a lid, their secrets they keep,
With shadows and giggles, they never sleep.
Each little seed dreams of grandiose plans,
But mostly enjoys, doing silly dance.

When the rain drops fall, the party begins,
Tiny raindrops spark laughter on skins.
They cheer 'More! More!' with jubilant cheer,
Growing their love, with hugs from here.

A Symphony of Sprouts

Gather 'round friends, for a concert today,
A symphony plays with the dirt and the clay.
Roots strumming softly, leaves tapping the beat,
The music of green makes life feel complete.

With pots as their stage, and light as the star,
Little plants hum—oh, how grand they are!
Each wiggle and jive in the bright sunny spots,
Plays a tune full of joy, in their tiny pots.

The Weight of a Leaf

A tiny leaf with dreams, so grand,
Hoping for a trip to a far-off land.
But the pot's too small, it barely can sway,
It giggles and whispers, 'I'll grow anyway!'

With a breeze, it flutters, a sight to behold,
In its little arena, feeling quite bold.
Yet every time it stretches for heights,
It flips upside down, oh what funny sights!

Each raindrop that falls is a rollercoaster,
The potted life is a merry jester.
'The world's my stage!' it chirps with glee,
But gets tangled in twigs, oh what irony!

So here it sits, in its cozy jail,
A leaf with ambitions, a fairy-tale tale.
While dreaming of forests, so lush and wide,
It dances and twirls, with roots that hide.

Echoes of the Subterranean

Down below, the whispers flow,
Muffled giggles in the dark below.
Tiny dwellers with dreams so vast,
Plotting their mischief, oh what a blast!

A worm claimed wisdom, a sage in dirt,
'There's freedom above - oh, isn't it absurd?'
But every time they peek up to see,
They stumble on each other – oh, what a spree!

Little ants in a line, they march so neat,
One trip on a root, and they all face defeat.
Hats off to the beetle that can't find its hat,
As it bumps 'round the garden exploring, how about that?

In this tiny realm, it's a party, you see,
With dance-offs and laughs, it's the place to be.
While dreaming of sunlight, they giggle with cheer,
Echoes of laughter, the underground sphere!

Petals of Potential

In a pot so small, the petals can't wait,
To burst forth in colors, not a moment too late.
But every time they try to unfurl,
They flop over sideways, oh what a swirl!

Each day they plot their escape with sass,
'We won't be contained, we'll break free at last!'
But the breeze whispers back, a chuckle so light,
'Think twice, dear petals, it's a bumpy flight!'

With a sunbeam's wink, they flutter and tease,
'Just a little more space, if you please!'
Yet each little blossom, so vivid and bright,
Gets tangled in sunshine, oh what a sight!

In this snug little pot, they bloom with a grin,
Determination's high, where will they begin?
With laughter and color, they outshine the rest,
Petals of potential, they're simply the best!

Dwarfed by Design

In a miniature realm where dreams take a pause,
The twigs and the buds seem to break all the laws.
A gnome in a garden, too proud to decay,
Wonders aloud, 'Is this all the play?'

Each flower too short, each leaf out of sight,
Yet they host a party, oh what pure delight!
With laughter and jesters, all bottle-sized,
Even squirrels are puzzled, quite mesmerized!

A tiny acorn flaunts its stature so small,
'The bigger, the better?' oh not at all!
With a twinkling laugh, it proclaims to the throng,
'This tiny brigade has been here all along!'

So here's to the small, the dwarfed and the bright,
In pots where they giggle, with all of their might.
While the world looms large, they have fun without care,
In a pint-sized party, where joy fills the air!

Tangles and Triumphs

In a pot that's hardly wide,
My plant does a game of hide.
With leaves that twist and turn,
I laugh as they seem to yearn.

A dance of vines, a playful mess,
Each leaf a fashionably dressed stress.
They reach for light, but oh so short,
In verdant dreams, they seek a court!

They tangle like spaghetti strands,
In tiny quarters, making plans.
While sipping sun, they prance about,
With little pot, they've no doubt!

In this confined, green jamboree,
They plot and schemed with glee.
So here's to plants with no real space,
Finding joy in their tiny race!

Distilled Beauty

In a pot, so snug and tight,
A plant with dreams takes flight.
With petals bright, it's quite the sight,
While giggling roots grab for the light.

Dancing leaves in a cramped abode,
Holding secrets no one's told.
In their tiny world, they make their mark,
With flair and fun, they spark a lark.

A leaf slips out, it takes a bow,
"Look at me!" it shouts, somehow.
Each inch a quest, each sprout a show,
In their little spot, they steal the glow!

So here's to plants with flair so fine,
In pots that barely let them shine.
They turn small spaces into fun,
Creating beauty, second to none!

Encased Aspirations

In a pot that's far too small,
My dreams of growth can only crawl.
Yet here they stand, so proud, so spry,
With tiny thoughts that reach the sky.

Wiggly stems in tight embrace,
Confinement's just a funny race.
With every leaf, they start to giggle,
In their little world, they dance and wiggle.

They stretch and twist, a playful feat,
In this little home, they won't face defeat.
They challenge size, with cheer and jest,
In tiny pots, they know they're blessed!

So raise a toast to dreams so bold,
In mini spheres, their tales unfold.
For even when the frames are tight,
Their spirits soar, a true delight!

Beyond the Rim

Peeking over the pot's high edge,
With glee, they form a leafy pledge.
With tiny limbs in great display,
They wave and cheer, "It's a good day!"

Like acrobats on a little stage,
They twist and turn, defy their cage.
With every soak, they laugh and play,
In their confined world, they steal the day!

The container shakes, they wobble, they shout,
"Make more room!" they squeal and pout.
But in this space, oh what a show,
With vibrant fun, they steal the glow!

So here we are, with plants so spry,
Finding joy as they reach high.
In pots too small, their fun persists,
With laughter and growth, they can't resist!

Little Wonders of Persistence

In a world so wide and vast,
Tiny dreams are growing fast.
A little sprout, a hopeful grin,
They stretch their leaves, they wiggle in.

With sun and care, they'll make their way,
In their cozy home, they want to stay.
A sprinkle here, a pinch of cheer,
A dance of joy—they're not in fear!

They twist and twirl, for all to see,
Little wonders, wild and free.
While bigger plants stand tall and grand,
These little ones have their own plan!

So here's to dreams in pots so small,
Who daringly embrace it all.
In their cramped space, they start to sing,
A chorus of hope in a tiny thing.

When Dreams Fit

In a pot that's snug, a dream takes form,
A sunshine smile in any storm.
With roots that wiggle, dance, and play,
They don't need much, just a bit of sway.

Funny how hopes can fit so tight,
Cramped and cozy, they're delight!
A seed once small, now large in mind,
In dreams we find what we'd call unlined.

As others grow, looking down with pride,
These pint-sized hopes won't be denied.
With every bud, they raise a toast,
To living large, they love it most!

So here's to dreams in cramped quarters,
Chasing sunlight like hoarding waters.
With giggles shared, they find their place,
In laughter's light, they leave a trace.

Threads of Life in a Cup

A cup of cheer, where dreams entwine,
Life threads in colors, so divine.
A sprinkle of laughter, a pinch of fun,
Tiny whispers of life, on the run.

Watch them flourish, these hopeful sights,
In little vessels, reaching heights.
With each new leaf, a tale is spun,
Of joy and mischief, blending as one.

The world may laugh at cups so small,
Yet here they thrive, they stand up tall.
With colors bright, they steal the show,
In this tiny life, there's room to grow!

So raise a cup to dreams that fit,
In pots and sips, they won't submit.
A toast to life—how sweet it is,
When joy pops up where chaos fizz!

Containered Dreams

In a clever pot, dreams dance about,
With wild ambitions, without a doubt.
They crammed their hopes like a joyful spree,
Knowing there's room for all to be free.

With laughter bubbling, they stretch so wide,
Inside this container, there's space for pride.
While skeptics chuckle, they don't seem phased,
These tiny dreams continue to blaze.

So here they are, all sassy and spry,
Dreams in a container, reaching for the sky.
With playful roots and giggles abound,
These fancy plants, they wear joy like a crown!

So let's not judge a cozy space,
Where dreams bloom sweetly, they find their place.
In pots so quaint, joy is alive,
In containered dreams, they truly thrive!

Daring to Bloom in Confinement

In a pot so small, yet dreams so tall,
Tiny sprouts shout, "We can have it all!"
With sunbeams dancing, they twist and they sway,
Pushing the limits in their own cheerful way.

Laughing at limits, they wiggle and stretch,
Who needs the forest? They're happy, they fetch.
With a splash of water, they giggle and grin,
In cramped little homes, they still crave to win.

Petite little leaves, they jive and they prance,
Daring the world to join in their dance.
A garden of misfits, all cozy and bright,
Challenging nature to give them a fright!

So here's to the sprigs, with gumption and flair,
In their playful pots, they have found their air.
No need for a wild, vast and open land,
For fun, they bloom, just as they had planned.

A World Encased

In a jar on the sill, a wonder unfolds,
Where tiny green dreams hold treasures untold.
Peaking through glass, they wave with delight,
"Look at us grow! Who needs space? We're alright!"

With each little stem, they muster their might,
Throwing a party in their cozy light.
"Might be a snug fit, but we're not here to pout,
We'll play hide and seek, and laugh all about!"

Soils from the backyard, and pebbles galore,
Mixing their skills, oh to dream and explore!
They giggle at daisies, both big and quite grand,
For royalty's here in their glass-walled land.

Twirling and swirling, their tiny leaves twine,
In their perfect domain, they sip lemonade fine.
Cheers to the plants that thrive in delight,
In worlds encased, they're shining so bright!

Nature's Cradle

In a cradle of clay, where sunbeams can peek,
Tiny ones nestle, all fuzzy and sleek.
With dreams made of pollen and joy in their veins,
They giggle together, despite tiny chains.

Sprouts dressed in green, they wiggle and sway,
Planning a heist for a grander bouquet.
Climbing the walls, they'll take on the stars,
Tiny superheroes, ignoring the bars!

With a sprinkle of charm and a dash of sass,
They plot like villains, their ambition amassed.
Who knew confinement could stir such a riot?
In nature's tight cradle, there's always a quiet!

Their world's a playroom, a jolly parade,
With each growing moment, new antics displayed.
In pots that may limit, their laughter spreads wide,
For joy carries weight, oh—nothing can hide!

Petals in the Shadows

In corners forgotten, where sunlight is rare,
Little blooms chuckle, they don't have a care.
"Shadows are cozy, why chase after light?
We'll dance in the gloom, and make our nights bright!"

With whispers of mischief, they plot their grand show,
Petals in twilight, they steal the night's glow.
"Who needs the spotlight? We'll sparkle from here,
Our quirky parade is the one you should cheer!"

A sprinkle of starlight, a dash of surprise,
Blooming in silence, they reach for the skies.
With giggles and wiggles, they sway with a grin,
In shadows, they fashion their own world within.

So here's to the petals, in dim-lit repose,
Crafting their magic where no one else goes.
With hearts ever hopeful, they charm through the dark,
Proving that laughter can bloom in the stark!

Microcosms of Natural Wonder

In a pot so small, my plant's quite bold,
It dreams of forests, or so I've been told.
With leaves so bright, it tries to play,
But trips on its tiny, leafy ballet.

A sunlight thief in a windowsill,
Stealing rays with an iron will.
With roots that dance in playful spins,
It giggles as it fights to win.

In this bustling home, it reigns supreme,
Claiming pot space like a leafy dream.
Its ambition's tall though its body's wee,
A tiny giant, oh can't you see?

Cactus in a cup, call it a sprite,
Daring rain clouds to give it a fright.
A snicker here, a sly grin there,
This nature's joke, for all to share.

Gardens in the Gaps

In the cracks of the pavement, a sprout peeks through,
With dreams of daisies; oh, how it grew!
Its pals are weeds with ambitions grand,
Taking over the yard, oh isn't it planned?

A flower in a teacup, oh what a sight,
Sipping on sunlight, drinking in light.
A tin can's a home for a curious sage,
With garden gnomes wondering how to engage.

Aiming for glory, it leaps with flare,
But who knew a plant could have such a dare?
It sways and it laughs in a charming parade,
In this odd little patch, nature's charade.

Tiny worlds bloom where no space exists,
With giggles from sprouts of nature's twist.
Scaling the walls, seeking the sun,
In gaps of our lives, they just want fun!

Suspended Growth

In a fishbowl, a plant takes a dip,
It dreams of the ocean, oh what a trip!
With roots in the air, it sways with grace,
Thinking it's found the perfect place.

A spider plant dangling, oh what a tease,
Turning heads with such effortless ease.
It swings in the breeze of a cool, soft fan,
Believing it's part of a great master plan.

Hydroponic heroes, such a delight,
Doing yoga at dawn, feeling so right.
With stems in the air, and no ground below,
They chuckle as other plants move so slow.

Each leaf a dancer in aerial space,
They laugh at their friends who have a slow pace.
In jugs and jars, the fun's just begun,
Suspended in time, chasing the sun!

A Breath of Green

In a shoe on a shelf, a herb starts to grow,
Pesto ambitions in its little show.
It dreams of pastas and pizza too,
Yet sits with a smile, enjoying the view.

Confined to tin cans, the sprouts have a ball,
Chattering and giggling, they stand up tall.
With colors so vibrant, they're quite the crew,
Turning heads in kitchens, oh what a view!

A tiny fern dressed up in a bow,
Sways in the jar, stealing the show.
Its friends, all faux plants, are green with envy,
As it pirouettes, feeling quite trendy.

So here's to the green in unexpected spots,
They tickle our fancies, forget-me-nots.
In laughter and joy, they spread their cheer,
A breath of green, oh, how delightful here!

Small Spaces, Great Journeys

In a corner, a plant with a dream,
Grows in a cup, plotting its scheme.
Tiny leaves waving, like they know,
Their travel plans are starting to show.

A sunflower whispers to a sweet pea,
"Look at us—so bold, yet so free!"
With no room to flop or to fall,
They dance in their spot, just having a ball.

A cactus jokes with a sprig of thyme,
"Who knew such fun could come from such grime?"
In their mini world, they're quite the affair,
Plant parties held in the thinnest of air.

Tiny pots with dreams big as the moon,
They'll conquer the wind, and hum a sweet tune.
With all of their quirks, they shine ever bright,
Who would have guessed they'd reach such a height?

Unfurling within Limits

With leaves poking out, a bid for the stars,
A busy fern whispers, "Excuse me, please, spars!"
In cramped little quarters, growth has some flair,
It's tough to be small, but we'll manage with care.

A tiny tomato, so proud of its size,
In a pint-sized cup, it's a king in disguise.
"I may be compact, but I'm ready to glow,
With all of this charm, who would ever say no?"

A leafy green marvel in a kiddie pool pot,
Says to its neighbors, "A party? Why not!"
They play in the sun, with jokes that are punny,
In this little patch, there's so much to be funny.

Though snug in their homes, they don't feel confined,
With each little stretch, a new joy they find.
Craving for space, but oh so content,
Making their mark with roots ever bent.

The Secret Life of Containers

Oh, the stories hidden in these little bowls,
Where plants engage in mischievous roles.
A pot of herbs laughs at the spice rack,
"In here, we simmer, and never lack!"

A saucer dreams of being a lake,
"I may just collect raindrops, oh what a break!"
While a humble clay pot wishes to roll,
"I'm boiling with charm, come witness my soul!"

The secret life of those who are barred,
Is one filled with fun, though their fate is marred.
When a gardener glances, they wink with delight,
"You think you're constrained? We're the proudest sight!"

A playful dance in an eight-inch sprawl,
Each plant saying, "We're having a ball!"
Together they giggle, enjoying their space,
In tiny containers, they flaunt their grace.

Nurture in a Narrow Niche

In a slim little nook, a flower takes stand,
It stretches out wide, though it's barely a hand.
"With just a few inches, I'll conquer the scene,
I'm the queen of this spot, you know what I mean!"

A mint leaf chuckles, "Hey, can you believe,
That in this wee world, we truly achieve?"
With sprigs so compact, they gather in cheer,
A garden of laughter is thriving right here!

They may not sprawl out or stretch to the sun,
But inside their chambers, they're having such fun.
With a flourish of green, they munch on their dreams,
In narrow confines, they burst at the seams!

Each pot is a universe, teeming with life,
Creating a buzz without causing strife.
"Nurture us close, we'll paint you our art,
In this narrow niche, we're happy to start!"

Unseen Connections

In a little pot on the windowsill,
The plants all joke about their thrill.
"Look at us, we're growing tall,"
While teasing each, they start to brawl.

"I'm the fern and you're just small,"
Said the cactus, feeling splendid, at all.
"But I've got spikes, and you just fluff,"
The debate rages, it's quite the guff.

"You got your shine, but I got the grit,"
Said the tiny succulents, just a bit.
Laughter echoes through the air,
Roots entwined, they're a quirky pair.

In their mini world, they play all day,
With dreams that dance and sway.
Tiny pots can hold such fun,
Who knew that growth could be a pun?

Embracing the Humble

Among the tiny plants so neat,
Life's lessons they can't defeat.
"I'm basic, but I like my place,"
Said the sprout with a little grace.

The others giggled, roots so fine,
In humble pots, they felt divine.
"I may be small, it's true, but wait,"
"My charm will surely resonate!"

"With water droplets, I'll make a splash,"
"In this tiny home, I'll make a dash."
They practice moves, tiny ballet,
Under the sun, they sway and play.

"We're the humble, we're the proud!"
They shout together, joyous and loud.
Life's a party in every nook,
Tiny pots filled with lots of rook!

Sprouts of Resilience

In a corner, so snug and tight,
The minis dance, what a sight!
"I'm tougher than I look,"
Said the sprout with quite a hook.

"With just a bit of sun and cheer,"
"I'll thrive right here, have no fear!"
A tiny laugh, a crooked leaf,
Turning struggles into a motif.

The herbs debate who's the best,
"I'm minty fresh—just smell my zest!"
"But I'm the basil, suave and sleek,"
In their tiny pots, they peak and squeak.

Resilience blooms in verdant hue,
In every sprout, a giggle or two.
The world should know their joyful roar,
In small containers, they're ready for more!

Whispered Dreams in miniature

In pots so small, dreams take their flight,
Whispers of green in the morning light.
"What if we could grow so high?"
Asked the thyme with a hopeful sigh.

"We'll make it big, yes, let's aspire!"
Said the little chives, lifting higher.
"With every drop of dew we drink,"
"World domination? Let's rethink!"

They share their hopes, giggles ensue,
"What if we were trees, quite the view?"
They burst with laughter, shaking their leaves,
Future fanciful, oh how it weaves!

In their tiny world, dreams are quite loud,
It's a secret club, oh so proud.
Plant friends united in laughter and schemes,
In miniature pots, they nurture their dreams!

Whispers of the Earth

In a pot so small, I stand,
Listening to whispers, oh so grand.
The dirt giggles, the leaves tease,
Hoping to grow as tall as trees.

A tomato once dreamed of a grand parade,
But found the sunlight just a charade.
In shadows, it pouts, wishing for room,
Small squabbles in dirt, sharing its gloom.

The herbs hold court, with sarcasm keen,
'We're the kings of this tiny scene!'
While weeds plot mischief, ready to spring,
Dancing in pots like it's spring-fling!

Yet tiny hearts bloom with glee,
Who knew such joy could fit in a spree?
In these small confines of laughter and jest,
Even little things can feel the zest.

Fragile Foundations

In a pot of dreams, I waddle and wiggle,
Cracks in the soil make me giggle.
Who knew a sprout could cause such a fuss?
I'm the star of this soil-stuffed bus!

With a leaf on my head, I strut with flair,
Hoping no one will notice my wear and tear.
'Look at me grow,' I boast with pride,
But deep down, I may need a wider ride.

The carrot's a storyteller, roots deep in lore,
While I'm here hoping for just a bit more.
'You think you're tough?' the radish sneers,
But I'm just a pot rebel, fueled by my fears.

As the sun sets on my tiny domain,
I dance in my pot, free of all strain.
Though fragile the ground, and silly the scene,
I'm thriving in chaos – the life of a bean!

The Secrets Beneath

In my tiny home, secrets grow,
What lurks below? Oh, who could know?
A scoop of soil hides dreams untold,
In whispers of roots, brave and bold.

Earthworms giggle, they wriggle with glee,
Countless adventures just under me.
'We've seen it all!' a critter will cheer,
'Just watch out for the rain, or things get smeared!'

A sprout plots a rise to the top of the shelf,
Dreaming of glory, thinking of self.
But a spider says, 'Stay put for a while,'
You'll be the star, just wait and smile.'

Each day, the soil holds laughter and light,
As petals and greens prepare for flight.
In this quirky realm, where dreams take flight,
The secrets beneath put worries to light.

Small Spaces, Big Dreams

In a little pot with dreams so huge,
I stretch my leaves, daring to fuse.
'Why so cramped?' the daisy asks me,
But small equals strength, just wait and see!

The thyme is sassy, the basil's a clown,
The ants hold court, wearing their crowns.
'In here, we're kings,' says a brave little sprout,
With laughter and banter, we dance all about!

As the sun peeks in, we bask in the glow,
In this playful pot, we steal the show.
A little bit wild, a whole lot of fun,
Even in limits, we still chase the sun!

So here's to the tiny, the dreams that we share,
In pots and in soil, there's magic to spare.
With giggles and glee, we embrace the charms,
In small spaces, we grow and cause alarms!

Nurtured in Scarcity

In a pot that's small and round,
Lies a sprout, snug and profound.
It dreams of fields and sunny skies,
Yet here it is, in its comical size.

Watered with care, it does its dance,
Straining to grow, given half a chance.
With a leaf that's tiny but quite the star,
It laughs at weeds, 'You won't go far!'

Dancing to roots that wiggle and play,
This cramped little patch brightens its day.
"Look at me!" it shouts with glee,
A giant in spirit, wild and free!

The Heart of a Seed

A little seed with big, bold dreams,
Hiding in soil, or so it seems.
Wishing for space where it can unwind,
But all it gets is a tiny bind.

"I'll stretch my leaves to touch the sky!"
It boasts to nearby ants passing by.
But in this pot, it takes a stand,
A stubborn little hero, oh so grand.

It giggles and wiggles in the warm sun,
"It's all for growth, just a bit of fun!"
Though cramped and snug with little flair,
This seedling knows it's got a rare air.

Little Homes for Boundless Dreams

In a pot with friends all stuck together,
These little sprouts hope for clear weather.
"Let's tell stories of gardens so wide,
Where we can roam and no one will chide!"

They huddle close in their cozy nook,
Each vivid leaf a well-thumbed book.
"Have you heard of the wind?" one whispers low,
"We could fly!" "Oh, please, let's give it a go!"

Though dreams are big and spaces small,
In their tiny homes, they stand proud and tall.
Laughing at giants in far-off lands,
They know together, they'll make amazing plans!

Unseen Life in Small Places

Just a pot on the sill, no one would guess,
A kingdom exists in this little mess.
"Did you pay rent?" the cactus jokes,
As the weeds share tales of funny pokes.

A tiny environment, a bustling hive,
They hold little parties, oh how they thrive!
With raindrops for music and sunlight for cheer,
Even a ladybug might swing by here!

In their cozy pot, they share their dreams,
Of vast horizons and life's lovely schemes.
Unseen by most, they giggle and play,
A merry bunch finding joy in the fray!

www.ingramcontent.com/pod-product-compliance
Lightning Source LLC
Chambersburg PA
CBHW072220070526
44585CB00015B/1420